REASON

By

Reverend David Peterson

Published by

KRATOS PUBLISHER

REASONS FOR MIRACLES

ISBN: 9781728782614

PUBLISHED BY
KRATOS PUBLISHERS

CONTENT PAGE

INTRODUCTION

The gospel of Luke is one of the synoptic Gospels and it was recorded by Luke who was a gentile. He was a medical doctor by profession, and worked and travelled with Paul.[1] There are many things that take place in this particular Gospel conveying the life and journey of Jesus via eye witness accounts (Luke 1:2). The Gospel is addressed to the most excellent Theophilus, who could have been someone of great influence and wealth. The reason for writing The Gospel and also the book of Acts was to convince Theophilus that the things He had been taught were most certainly true (Luke 1:4). Luke-Acts has traditionally been regarded as the gospel for the Gentiles, with the language, through-patterns and Theological resources of Hellenistic Judaism.[2] Though I believe Luke planned his two books together, with the result that they have cross-referencing and modifications both from the Gospel to Acts and from Acts to the Gospel, it seems quite plausible that the actual writing and appearance of the two volumes may have been separated by some time, as is often the case

---

[1] Ibojie 2009, 175
[2] FletcHer-Louis 1997, 18

4

with multi-volume works. [3] I am focusing on how Luke used the scriptures of Israel for shaping of his narrative, not the interpretations of specific passages, though certainly Luke's own inter-textual use of the Scriptures of Israel has an 'exegetical' element. [4] In this extended essay one will convey some of the reasons why Jesus performed miracles according to The Gospel of Luke.

Luke, like all of The Gospels, is a story told from faith to faith.[5] The Gospel of Luke starts with the miraculous conceptions of Elizabeth the mother of John the Baptist who was barren and the mother of Jesus, Mary, who was a virgin. He then conveys The genealogy of Jesus in chapter 2 and writes about Jesus being aware of his vocation at The young age of 12, where He is in The temple and declares to his parents that He must be about his Father's business (Lk 2:49). Jesus is then baptised and led by the Spirit to be tempted by the devil in the wilderness. The devil then tries to entice Jesus into performing miracles and worshiping Him for political positions of power.

---

[3] Kurz 1993, 22
[4] Litwak 2005, 48
[5] Ringe 1995, 5

Jesus rejected the way of flaunting miracles and He will not take up the political sword.[6] At this point He has overcome the temptation of the adversary and is now ready to start His ministry.

---

[6] Craddock 2009, 57

FULFILLING PROPHECY

Jesus begins to perform signs, wonders and miracles by first casting out a demon in Luke 4:35. He then Heals the mother in law of Peter 4:39 and heals many who were sick and cast out many demons in Luke 4:40-41. One could say one of the reasons Jesus did miracles is located just before Luke writes Him performing the miracle in the passages just mentioned. this is located in Luke 4:18-21 where Jesus reads Isaiah 61:1-2a in the synagogue in His home town of Nazareth. The Passage in Isaiah 61:1-2a states:

'The Spirit of The Lord is upon me, because He hath anointed me to preach The gospel to The poor; He hath sent me to Heal The broken Hearted, to preach deliverance to The captives, and recovering of sight to The blind, to set at liberty Them that are bruised, to preach The acceptable year of The Lord.'

The themes in this passage of joy, blessing, the vindication of the oppressed, and the fulfilment of divine promises are consistent throughout Luke's Gospel, and thus the words of blessing sound a keynote for the evangelist.[7] After He reads this He states in Luke 4:21 'This day is

---

[7] Tiede 1988, 51-52

7

this scripture fulfilled in your ears.' The reaction of the people comes across as very alarming as Jesus is taken out of the synagogue by them and they attempt to throw off the side of the cliff. At this point Jesus realises that a prophet is without honour in his home town and the fact that the people who He had grown up with were so familiar with Him, They found it hard to believe that the scripture from Isaiah He had read could possibly be related to Him in any shape or form. They found what He was saying so blasphemous that they made this drastic attempt to end His life. How He disappears through the crowd is a miracle in itself and one would say He performed this as it was not yet his time to die. The words of the prophet Isaiah cited in Luke 4: 18-19 declare why the Holy Spirit is so intimately connected to Jesus. It is the Spirit that has empowered an enabled Jesus to fulfil God's plan for Him as revealed in the prophecy of Isaiah.[8] So one would say that one of the reasons Jesus Performed Miracles was to fulfil prophecy.

---

[8] Nave 2002, 21

PLAN AND PURPOSE

The next miracle Jesus performs according to The Gospel of Luke is the miraculous catching of a multitude of fish. This takes place in Luke 5:4-6 where Jesus advises Peter to cast his nets into the deeper side of the sea. Although Peter was a professional fishermen and had been fishing all night he obeyed Jesus and he miraculously caught so much fish that, on verse 6 and 7 states the fishing nets began to rip and they needed to get another boat to carry the weight of the fish, as the weight was so great the boats began to sink. Peter then tells Jesus that he is a sinful man and that Jesus should depart from Him, as the miracle was so great he recognised that Jesus was no ordinary man. But Jesus states in

 Luke 5:10b 'Fear not; from Henceforth thou shalt catch men.'

Luke 5:10b (KJV)

Other translations say that he will become a fisher of men. So one would say that one of the reasons Jesus did miracles was to show and display to His followers the *plan and purpose* He had for their lives.

MESSIANIC SECRET

The following miracle Jesus performs is the healing of the man with leprosy. This occurs in Luke 5:12-14 where a man full of leprosy falls on the ground before Jesus and says to Him 'Lord, if you are willing, make me clean. Jesus responds in verse 13 and says 'I am willing, be clean.' He then instructs the leaper to show Himself to the priest as stated in the Law of Moses. Lepers are excluded from association with other people because of their disease and unclean status before God (Leviticus 14-15), but in Jesus' ministry they are cleansed (5:12-16).[9] Looking at this passage of scripture, one would say that one of the reasons why Jesus did miracles was out of His own personal will.

In verse 14 He also tells the man with leprosy not to disclose the fact that Jesus had performed the miracle. This is referred to as **"The messianic secret"**. Many say He wanted this secret to be kept because He wanted to avoid conflict with the religious leaders or that He didn't want to be a celebrity, so He could move around with ease. And there is a theological explanation, that it was not yet the proper time for Him to be revealed as The

---

[9] Green 1995, 63

Messiah.[10] Even though He would tell those He healed not to say anything Luke 5:15 states that His fame still grew, which caused many to come to Him for healing and miracles. So one would say that one of the reasons Jesus did miracles was because of how quickly his fame spread, attracting those that need a miracle.

---

[10] Ashcraft 2016, 7

MANIFESTED AUTHORITY

The next miracle Jesus did was the healing of the paralytic. This happens in Luke 5:17-24. The man being paralysed from the neck down was being carried around by his four friends and the facility Jesus was in was packed to capacity. Luke and Matthew in comparison do not go into much detail on how the man was brought to Jesus. But Mark goes as far as to say that the friends who carried the paralytic made a hole in the roof to lower the bed with the paralytic on it. This miracle again fails to be mentioned in The Gospel of John.

When Jesus saw this He told the man that his sin had been forgiven, which caused contention between Jesus and the religious leaders and they said within themselves that only God is able to forgive sins. Jesus, in response to their thoughts as stated in Luke 5:23-24 said to the religious leaders:

'Which is easier to say, 'Get up and walk'? But I want you to know that the Son of Man has authority on earth to forgive sins.' So He said to the paralyzed man, 'I tell you, get up, take your mat and go home.'

Luke 5:23 -24 (KJV)

According to the Gospel of Luke Jesus has performed this miracle in order to show the authority that He carries as the Son of Man to forgive sins, as stated in verse 24 of the fifth chapter.

THE SABBATH

In chapter six Jesus performs a miracle on the Sabbath. The Sabbath provides yet another occasion for a miracle of Jesus which again benefits someone who is weak.[11] This adds to the contention between Jesus and the religious leaders as the Jews are supposed to rest on The Sabbath and are not to perform any works. However, Jesus asks a rhetorical question in Luke 6:9 which say:

'Then said Jesus unto them, I will ask you one thing; is it lawful on the Sabbath days to do good, or to do evil? To save life, or to destroy it?'

Luke 6:9 (KJV)

He then heals the man with the withered arm which sparks the plot for the religious leaders to kill Him. One would say the reason Jesus performed this miracle was to do good to the man with the withered arm as posed in His rhetorical question. Also one would say that He wanted to develop the minds of the people into understanding that God is not interested in legalism as much as He is restoration. One

---

[11] O' Toole 1984, 36

would say Jesus came to change this mind-set, as people were tired of dead religion.[12]

COMPASSION

Chapter 7:11-15 Jesus raises the young man, from Nain, from the dead. Jesus comes to Nain and witnesses a weeping mother carrying her son in a coffin. This miracle only appears in The Gospel according to Luke and no other Gospel. The raising of the widow's son at Nain recalls Elijah's similar miracle (Lk. 7.11-17, cp 1 Kings 17.17-24). [13] One would say the reason why Jesus performed this miracle is located in verse 13 which states: And when the Lord saw her , He had compassion on her, and said unto her, weep not.' So one would say the reason why Jesus performed this miracle according to The Gospel of Luke, was because He was moved by compassion

---

[12] Alexander 2009, 133
[13] Burridge 2005, 111

SURPRISING FAITH

The following miracle was the healing of the centurion's servant. This takes place in Capernaum as Jesus enters He is informed of the centurion's love for the nation of Israel as he built a synagogue for them to worship in. On his way to the centurion's house Jesus is approached by friends of the centurion who relay a message to Jesus in regards to His authority as the Messiah and Saviour. Luke notes that the centurion, having heard of Jesus, regards Him as a saviour (for healers were often regarded as "saviours" in Roman antiquity) to whom He had no immediate access.[14] The centurion recognises that Jesus is a man of authority and asks Jesus to just speak the word and his servant will be healed. The centurion compared this to when he would send forth a command and his servants would obey. So He believed so much in the spiritual authority of Jesus, that he believed that Jesus could heal his servant by simply speaking a command for the healing to transpire.

---

[14] Green 1997, 279

Even Jesus was surprised at the amount of faith the centurion displayed and states in Luke 7:9b

'I say unto you, I have not found so great faith, no, not in Israel.'

Luke 7:9b (KJV)

One would say some of the reasons why Jesus did miracles was because of the suggestion of the Jewish people, a sign of his spiritual authority and the surprising faith people who are gentiles conveyed.

DEMONS AND STORMS

In the Gospel of Luke Chapter eight, here we see that Jesus has chosen all twelve of His disciples and He is going from village to village preaching and sharing good tiding of the Kingdom of God (Luke 8:1). In verse two the Gospel speaks of Jesus casting out seven devils from Mary Magdalene. Some scholars would argue that Mary Magdalene was the very first Apostle. As she was the first to encounter the risen Jesus and was sent by Him to tell the disciple that Jesus is not dead but that He has surely risen. One would say that Jesus cast the demons out of Mary Magdalene because He knew her purpose and destiny. And in order for her to fulfil it she had to become set free from demonic oppression.

Chapter 8:22-25 Jesus performs the miracle of calming the storm. In Matthew and Mark the story of this miracle storm is pretty much the same but the story is not mentioned in John as John has always been seen as the odd one out in regards to the Gospels, with a more unique purpose. This was due to the fact that as Jesus and the disciples were on their way to the country of the Gardarenes a storm arose and this caused the disciple to panic, as it was a very violent and horrific storm. At the time Jesus was asleep. So the disciples woke Him up to inform Him that they were about to die due to the raging storm. Jesus gets up and rebukes the storm and the storm settled. At this time Jesus then asked the disciples the question where is your faith? (Luke 8:25). One would say the reason Jesus perform this miracle was due to the lack of faith of the disciples. One would say that this was a huge sign of the divine nature of Jesus being put on display. The hypostatic union between Him and the Father was very much conveyed through this miracle.

As the forces of nature throughout time and history have never been able to be controlled by man. It has always been in relation to divine beings and Jesus displaying this much power, showing that He truly was God manifested on the earth. Even the disciples were afraid at this display of power as the scripture states in Luke 8:25b

'......And they being afraid wondered, saying one to another, what manner of man is this! For He commands even the winds and water, and they obey Him.'

Luke 8:25b (KJV)

The following miracle Jesus performs was the casting out of Legion. The in-depth description of this miracle is found in Mark 5:1-20.

Matthew and Luke give a similar description and this miracle fails to appear in the Gospel of John. We see here Jesus meeting a man who is possessed by a multitude of demons, who is cutting himself with stones and braking chains that was placed on him by the towns people. As Jesus is casting out the demons, the demons negotiate with Jesus so He could allow them to go into a herd of pigs. As the demons enter the pigs, the pigs throw themselves off a cliff. This causes the towns people to ask Jesus to leave as they found the whole encounter extremely frightening and uncomfortable.

When looking at this narrative, one would assume that the reaction of the towns people would not be so. One would think that after they had witnessed and heard of this great display off power and glory of God, that they would have accepted Jesus into their land with open arms. But instead they reject and sent Him away as the act that Jesus committed broke their flow of normalcy and cause an up raw.

One would say that this may have been due to the financial loss because of the amount pigs that headed off the cliff. Or it may have been due to the fact that the towns people were just not use to this level of spiritual activity taking place in their area. As Jesus and the disciples were leaving, The man that had been set free from demonic possession ran up to Jesus, and asked if he could follow Him. Jesus told him to stay behind and declare what God has done for him (Luke 8:39). One would say the reason behind Jesus performing this miracle was to start the evangelistic ministry of the young man who was possessed, so that the message of God's greatness can go forth and spread amongst the area.

FAITH AND HUMILITY

The next miracle that Jesus performs is that of the Healing of the woman with the issue of blood. Again Matthew and Luke's description of this story is similar whereas, Mark goes more into detail. Most scholars agree that Mark's Gospel was The first and Matthew and Luke's came after and that Matthew and Luke get a lot of their material from an unknown source referred to as 'Q.' This takes place in Luke 8:43-48. Jesus is on his way to the house of Jairus who was a ruler of the synagogue, to heal his daughter who was on the verge of death.

As He went, a woman who had an irregular menstrual cycle grabbed the ends of his robe and became healed of her issue. She had so much faith in the ministry of Jesus that she believed if she touched His garment she would be made whole. Jesus asked His disciple's if they knew who touched Him. As there were a lot of people around Him they couldn't tell Him. One would say that this lady through faith was able to tap into his divinity.

A human is virtuous through hard work; the gods, however, are virtuous simply because of who they are.'[15] She drew upon His virtue and power without Him even being aware, which caused Him to stop and find out who touched Him. Until the lady confessed and He says to her in verse 48: *Daughter, be of good comfort: thy faith hath made thee whole; go in peace.* One would say that according to the gospel of Luke this miracle took place in the ministry of Jesus because of the faith of the woman with the issue of blood. Following this incident Jesus eventually makes it to the house of Jairus and his daughter is pronounced dead.

Jesus Then clears the room and only allows three disciples and the parent of the young lady to be in the room. The reason why one would say Jesus brought her back to life and performed this tremendous miracle was because Jarius had humbled himself, bowed down before Jesus and pleaded for Him to do so which occurs in Luke 8:41.

---

[15] McConnell 2014, 50

MULTIPLICATIONS

The next Miracle is the only miracle Jesus performs that is mentioned in all four gospels. This is the feeding of the 5000 men plus women and children. In Mark, Matthew and Luke Jesus looks up to Heaven give thanks and breads the bread whereas, in John He just gives thanks. But they are all consistent in the fact that Jesus did some form of prayer before performing this miracle. Theissen observed that Luke on three occasions records that Jesus prayed shortly before divine power was manifested through or in Him.[16]

As this seemed to be the most popular miracle this was defiantly one of those times. This happens in Luke 9:10-17 where Jesus had just finished ministering and as time had gone, He wanted to feed the people as it was late in the evening. The disciples could only present two fish and five loaves of bread before Jesus. So He prayed over the food and shared it out to the point that He was able to feed this great number of people.

---

[16] Marshall 1992, 555

Where his story runs parallel to Matthew and Mark, Luke adds a reference to prayer on no fewer than eleven occasions.[17] One would say that the reason why Jesus performed this miracle was to feed the people and also it was the result of strong, fervent prayer.

---

[17] Motyer 2000, 11

TRANSFIGURATION TO DELIVERANCE

Luke 9:37-43 we see Jesus coming down from a mountain with Peter, James and John. This is the mount of transfiguration where Jesus display His true form to the disciples that He trusted the most out of the twelve. On the mountain He meets Moses and Elijah. One representing the Law and the other the prophets. As they discuss Jesus' mission and His preparation for it. When they get to the bottom the other disciples are faced with a situation where in which they are unable to cast out a demon from a young man. The father of the young man runs to Jesus and asks Him to deliver his son from the evil spirit. Jesus has a moment of frustration and states in verse 41: O faithless and perverse generation, how long shall I be with you, and suffer you? Bring thy son hither.' This showed his frustration which led to Him mentioning his death for the first time in Luke in verse 44. One would say the reason for Jesus performing this miracle was out of frustration.

Jesus then heals a blind mute demoniac and is accused by the religious leaders of using demonic spirits to perform miracles. Jesus then breaks down how the devils kingdom works and how one cannot cast out demons using the power of the devil, as the kingdom of darkness is not divided. He causes us to know that the kingdom of darkness doesn't operate via chaos and confusion. This conveys that the kingdom of darkness operate via order and rank and that one who casts demons out, cannot be doing this via the power of the devil but only by the power of God. The demonstration of such supernatural power is one aspect of the fingerprint of God.[18] As Jesus states in Luke 11:20: 'But if I with the finger of God cast out devils, no doubt the kingdom of God is come upon you.' One would say that the reason Jesus casts out this demon according to the book of Luke is to show that the Kingdom of God has come through Him.

---

[18] Geisler 1988, 26

TRADITION VS MIRACLES

The plot thickens in the gospel of Luke 13:11-17 as Jesus does another healing on the Sabbath to display the true meaning of the day, as it is a day of rest and not of bondage. This miracle only appears in Luke's gospel and isn't mentioned in any of the others. A woman, who was bent over for eighteen years, was seen by Jesus as she entered the temple. Jesus spoke over her and told her she was loosed from her infirmity, laid hands on her and immediately she was made straight. This upset the ruler of the synagogue as Jesus healed on the Sabbath.

So the ruler of the synagogue tells the people to come on another day of the week for healing but not on the Sabbath. This seems to be a constant theme in Luke's Gospel, where Jesus would follow the culture of The kingdom of God rather than the religious protocol of the Jewish traditions. Jesus responds in verse 15-16 which states:

The Lord then answered Him, and said, Thou hypocrite, doth not each one of you on the

Sabbath loose his ox or his ass from the stall, and lead Him away to watering?

And ought not this woman, being a daughter of Abraham, whom Satan hath bound, lo, these eighteen years, be loosed from this bond on the Sabbath day?

Luke 13:15-16 (KJV)

Jesus referring to her as a daughter of Abraham shows how much He was trying to get the point across that the woman was like family to their community and still they were willing to allow their wrongly interpreted tradition and ritual to get in the way of allowing her to be set free. Eighteen years of suffering was a long time for one to be in this state. This would have left the woman depressed, lonely and down trodden.

The religious leaders failed to understand why Jesus was so bold as to break protocol and how He would have no regards for the traditions they had been practicing for generations. This came across as an undermining of their authority, power and position, which caused them to feel so uneasy and less settled. So the ruler of the synagogue and all the religious leaders that hated Jesus and were put to shame and all the people began to worship God. One would say Jesus performed this miracle because of the level of affliction the woman had suffered. Also to contest the Jewish traditions.

In Luke 14:1-6 Jesus heals again on the Sabbath in the house of one of the chief Pharisees. This miracle is only mentioned by Luke and none of the other Gospels. He heals a man with dropsy which now a days would be called "oedema". This takes place right in house of the chief priest who is fully opposed to any form of healing being done on the Sabbath. So one could imagine the tense atmosphere as this miracle is about to take place.

Before healing the man Jesus asks all who were in the house if it is lawful for Him to heal on the Sabbath. As nobody answered, one could imagine the awkward silence that must of took place in that moment. As if to say that Jesus knowing full well that the majority of the people sitting in the house doesn't agree with what He is going to do. But that didn't stop Him as Jesus healed the man who was sick with dropsy and addressed the hypocrisy of the Pharisees.

He mentioned what He said previously in the Gospels and repeats it in verse 5. That the religious leaders still tend to their animals for their own self gain on the Sabbath, but have issues with Jesus wanting to heal and set people free on that day. One would say the reason why Jesus did this miracle was to help the man and to address the hypocrisy of the religious leaders.

LEPROSY DEFEATED

The next miracle that took place was the healing of the ten lepers. This occurred in Luke's Gospel 17:12-19. Jesus is approached by the ten lepers and as He is approached the ten lepers lift up their voices and ask Jesus to show mercy on them. So Jesus tells them to show themselves to the Priest. As they are going they notice that their leprosy begins to disappear. One returns to say thank you and give God praise. Jesus was shocked that out of nine only one returned to say thank you and to give God praise. He was even more shocked that the one that returned wasn't even a Jew but a Samaritan.

The Samaritans were people who were rejected and despised by the Jews as they were half Jewish and half Samarian. So they were children born out of the time Samaria enslaved Israel. So their existence was connected to a horrible time in the history of the Israelites Hence why they were so hated. Jesus' expectation had not been met by the lepers especially those who were of Jewish decent. As they would have been aware of the level of rejection they would have had to be expose to due to the law of Moses. As they were all healed one would have expected all them to come back and say thank you to God, or at least four or five of them as the experience of having leprosy living in that society was catastrophic. He then declares to the leper, that his faith has made him whole. One would say that the reason they were healed was because they cried out. Also the one that was made whole was made whole because of his curtsey to say thank you and as Jesus stated it was also because of his faith.

OPTICAL PHENOMENON

The next miracle that takes place is found in Luke 18:35-43 where Jesus heals a blind man by the way side begging. Matthew and Luke don't mention the name of the blind man. We only see this in the Gospel of Mark 10: 46 which states: 'And they came to Jericho and as He went out of Jericho with His disciples and a great number of people, blind Bartimaeus, the son of Timaeus, sat by the highway side begging.' The blind man heard all the commotion and asked what was happening. When the people told him, he began to cry out for Jesus to help him. As he cried out the people around him told him to be quiet. But the more they told him to be quiet, the louder he became. Jesus Then asked him to be brought to Him and healed him of his blindness.

As he cried out he referred to Jesus as the son of David. This was a messianic cry which displays that he had believed Jesus to be the Messiah and the chosen one of Israel. The fact that the man was blind and Jesus heals him, was a messianic prophecy being fulfilled by

Jesus as The Prophet Isaiah say in Isaiah 35: 4-5 which states: *Say to Them that are of a fearful Heart, be strong, fear not: behold, your God will come with vengeance, even God with a recompense; He will come and save you. Then eyes of the blind shall be opened, and The ears of the deaf shall be opened, and the ears of the deaf shall be unstopped.*' One would say that the reason this miracle happens was because the blind man had a relentless attitude to towards getting the attention of Jesus and it was a sign of Jesus fulfilling messianic prophecies.

HEALING EARS

That last miracle Jesus performed before His death, burial and resurrection was the restoration of the soldier's ear. This takes place Luke 22:50-51. One of the disciples takes up a sword and cuts the ear of one of the soldiers that came to arrest Jesus. Jesus then heals the solider and asks the religious leaders if they were coming to arrest a thief, due to the fact that they had to bring so many soldiers with them. It was a criminal offense and punishable by death for one to wound a soldier. Jesus healing the soldier's ear was Jesus getting rid of the evidence. If Jesus had not healed the ear, then the disciple would have been tried and put to death, before his time. Now The Gospel of Luke does not say which disciple it is. However according to the Gospel of John it was Simon Peter, which raises the stakes even higher. As Simon being the one to lead the birth of the church in such a profound way in the book of acts. For Him to be arrested and put to death would have been catastrophic for the plans Jesus had for His church to move forward after He had returned back to his Father in heaven. One would say that Jesus healed the solider to protect the disciple that struck his ear as this could of led them to being put to death, which would have affected the plan for the message of Jesus to blossom into the world. Finally, we must note how brilliantly Luke has woven this episode into the total structure of his work.' [19] He displayed one more tie of the great Healing miracle working power of Jesus just as He is emerging unto The grand stage of the trail, death and resurrection.

[19] Wilson 1973, 137

CONCLUSION

In conclusion there are many reasons why Jesus did miracles. The fact that Luke is a doctor by profession, one would think that he would have the most miracles documented in his Gospel but it is actually Mark. The Gospel of Luke takes its time to tell this amazing story of Jesus and is often described as the Gospel for the poor and marginalised. But one would say that the main reason Jesus did miracles was because of who He was. He's compassionate, prayerful and at times even frustrated. But all these elements made up the character of a loving saviour of the world. The religious leaders throughout the Gospel tried to display God through their dead traditions. But when Jesus came, He said; *'If you want to know what God is like, look at me.'*[20]

He time and time again healed on the Sabbath day to show that God is more concerned about Helping people, than He is about tradition, rituals and festivals. One would think this may have come from Luke

---

[20] Barclay 2001, 163

experiencing rejection in the contentions scenes in the book of Acts between the Jewish Christians and the Gentile Christians. Luke being a Gentile consistently shows how much Jesus was opposed to this showing that the Gospel message was not just for Israel but for the world. He did miracles to show that through Him, The culture of the kingdom of God had come amongst the people. That God Himself had come down in human form. That their long awaited Messiah had arrived to live out God divine plan and bring salvation to the world.

He inspired people to realise their calling and set them free from demonic oppression, sickness and disease. But ultimately Jesus did miracles because He cared. In pouring out His energy and compassion on behalf of the poor and the sick, Jesus the servant prepared for his own death.[21] He displayed great qualities of a servant king.

---

[21] Senior 1992, 23

BIBLIOGRAPHY

Alexander. P. 2009. *Signs and Wonders: Why Pentecostalism is The World's Fastest Growing Faith.* San Francisco: Jossey-Bass A Wiley Imprint.

Barclay. W. 2001. *The Gospel of Luke.* Louisville: Westminster John Knox Press.

Burridge. R. A. 2005. *Four Gospel, One Jesus?* London: Society for Promoting Christian Knowledge.

Craddock. F. B. 2009. *Luke.* Louisville: Westminster John Knox Press.

Davila-Ashcraft. J. 2016. *The Messianic Secret: Discovering The Lost Years and True Identity of Jesus.* USA: Paleo-Orthodox Publishing.

FletcHer-Louis. C. H. T. 1997. *Luke-Acts: Angels, Christology and Soteriology.* Tubingen: Mohr Siebeck.

Geisler. N. 1988. *Signs and Wonders.* Portland: Wjpf and Stock PublisHers.

Green. J. B. 1997. *The Gospel of Luke.* Cambridge: Wm. B. Eermans Publishing.

Green. J. B. 1995. *The Theology of The Gospel of Luke.* Cambridge: Cambridge University Press.

Holy Bible.

Ibojie. J. 2009. *Bible-Based Dictionary of PropHetic Symbols for Every Christian.* Aberdeen: Christian Book PublisHers.

Kurz. W. S. 1993. *Reading Luke-Acts: Dynamics of Biblical Narrative.* Louisville: Westminster John Knox Press.

Litwak. K. D. 2005. *Echoes of Scripture in Luke-Acts: Telling The History of God's People Intertextually.* New York: T&T Clark International.

Marshall. H. I, Green. J. B and McKnight. S. Eds. 1992. *Dictionary of Jesus and The Gospels.* Illinois: Inter Varsity Press.

McConnell. J. R. 2014. *The topos of Divine Testimony in Luke-Acts.* Portland: Wipf and Stock PublisHers.

Motyer. S. 2000. *New Testament Introduction.* Singapore: Candle books.

Nave. G. D. 2002. *The Role and Function of Repentance in Luke-Acts.* Boston: Society of Biblical Literature.

O' Toole. R. F. 1984. *The unity of Luke's Theology: An Analysis of Luke-Acts.* Portland: Wipf and Stock PublisHers.

Ringe. S. H. 1995. *Luke.* Louisville: Westminster John Knox Press.

Senior. D. 1992. *The Passion of Jesus in The Gospel of Luke.* Minnesota: The Liturgical Press.

Tiede D. L. 1988. *Luke.* Minneapolis: Augsburg Publishing House.

Wilson. S. G. 1973. *The Gentiles and The Gentile Mission in Luke-Acts.* New York: Cambridge University Press.

37398466R00024

Printed in Great Britain
by Amazon